STU

GOD IN
THE PSALMS

by
Carol Veldman Rudie

CRC Publications
Grand Rapids, Michigan

Unless otherwise noted, Scripture quotations in this publication are
from the HOLY BIBLE, NEW INTERNATIONAL VERSION, © 1973,
1978, 1984, International Bible Society. Used by permission of
Zondervan Bible Publishers.

Cover photo by PhotoDisc.

Discover Your Bible series. Discover God in the Psalms, © 1988, 2000,
CRC Publications, 2850 Kalamazoo Ave. SE, Grand Rapids, MI 49560.
All rights reserved. Printed in the United States of America on recycled
paper. ✪ We welcome your comments. Call us at 1-800-333-8300 or
e-mail us at editors@crcpublications.org.

ISBN 1-56212-194-4

10 9 8 7 6 5 4 3

Contents

How to Study

The questions in this study booklet will help you discover for yourself what the Bible says. This is inductive Bible study—no one will tell you what the Bible says or what to believe. You will discover the message for yourself.

Questions are the key to inductive Bible study. Through questions you will search for the writers' thoughts and ideas. The prepared questions in this booklet are designed to help you in your quest for answers. You can and should ask your own questions too. The Bible comes alive with meaning for many people as they discover for themselves the exciting truths it contains. Our hope and prayer is that this booklet will help the Bible come alive for you.

The questions in this study are designed to be used with the New International Version of the Bible, but other translations can also be used.

Step 1. Read the Bible passage several times. Allow the thoughts and ideas to sink in. Think about its meaning. Ask questions of your own about the passage.

Step 2. Answer the questions, drawing your answers from the passage. Remember that the purpose of the study is to discover what the Bible says. Write your answers in your own words. If you use Bible study aids such as commentaries or Bible handbooks, do so only after completing your own personal study.

Step 3. Apply the Bible's message to your own life and world. Ask yourself these questions: What is this passage saying to me? How does it challenge me? Comfort me? Encourage me? Is there a promise I should claim? A warning I should heed? For what can I give thanks? If you sense God speaking to you in some way, respond to him in a personal prayer.

Step 4. Share your thoughts with someone else if possible. This will be easiest if you are part of a Bible study group that meets regularly to share discoveries and discuss questions. If you would like to learn of a study group in your area or if you would like more information on how to start a small group Bible study, write to Discover Your Bible, 2850 Kalamazoo Ave. SE, Grand Rapids, MI 49560 or to P.O. Box 5070, STN LCD 1, Burlington, ON L7R 3Y8.

Introduction

You are embarking on a study of the character of God. In this study you will explore the Psalms—songs written by God's people as cries for help, as songs of exultant praise, as quiet meditations on God's power and love. You will sense the depth of the psalm writers' knowledge of God's character. They will speak to you of God's steadfast love, immeasurable power, and unchanging faithfulness.

As you study, remember that you are working with poetry. Poets often use images—word pictures to describe something. These psalms liken God to many things—a thunderstorm, a father with small children, a king, a rock of refuge, and so on. Let the imagery come alive for you; play with the word pictures and try to sense the emotions and feelings behind them. To the ancient Hebrews, one picture was better than a thousand words. You will see why as you begin to work with poetry that has been preserved for hundreds of years.

The handful of psalms you will study in this series look at God's character from many different perspectives: as Creator, as compassionate Father, as reigning King, as faithful Lover, as righteous Lord, as the one true God, and as the God who calls people to a saving relationship with himself. These psalms will challenge the ways you've always thought about God. They will deepen your understanding of who God is, what God has done in history, and how God works in our lives today. The songs written by the people of God centuries ago still speak with fresh insight about the one thing that remains unchanging in an unstable world: the character of God.

Glossary of Terms

angels—heavenly beings created by God as messengers to carry out his will in the world and to serve and care for those who belong to God.

Asaph—one of the chief musicians appointed by King David to supply the music and compose the songs used in the worship of the Lord.

cedars of Lebanon—the greatest of trees in the Near East; a metaphor for the richness of creation.

covenant—a mutually binding agreement between two parties. Early in Israel's history, God had promised to be a God to the Israelites if they would obey his laws and worship only God.

cup of salvation—most likely the cup of wine drunk at the festal meal that served as the climax of a thank offering. The sacrifice and its meal celebrated deliverance by the Lord.

David—the second king of Israel, beloved by God for his faithfulness to God's will, a military genius, and the ancestor to the line of kings that ruled throughout the Old Testament.

Desert of Kadesh—an arid region in the north of Israel.

enemies—people who oppose God and persecute his people.

Father—name for God used by Jesus.

fear of the Lord—awe of God's power and holiness, combined with love for God and obedience to his will.

gods—objects of worship (idols or the powers represented by idols) other than the Lord, the true God.

heaven—the place where God lives.

holiness—pure; set apart in a special way to bring glory to God.

holy—perfect in goodness and righteousness; pure; set apart in a special way to bring glory to God.

Holy One—another name for God. "Holy" here means being perfect in goodness and righteousness.

images—another word for idols.

Israel—the name God gave to the Old Testament patriarch Jacob and to all his descendants who are the people of God.

Jacob—one of the patriarchs whose descendants became the people of Israel. He was given the name Israel by God, and was revered as one of the spiritual and physical fathers of the Israelite nation.

Jesus Christ the Righteous One—Jesus is the Messiah, a Hebrew word translated Christ, the person who is completely right with God.

leviathan—a fearsome mythological monster of the deep.

LORD—the personal name by which God made himself known to the Israelites.

lyre—a hand-held, harp-like instrument often used to accompany singing.

Moses—the man God chose to lead the people of Israel out of Egypt to the borders of Canaan. During his leadership he received from God and taught Israel the laws that would govern them as God's chosen people.

Most High—name for God.

oracle—usually refers to words of revelation from God—for example, words spoken by the prophets.

pit—used to trap wild animals or for food storage.

psalm—a Hebrew poem designed for use in worship; often sung.

sacrifice—the act of offering something precious to God, usually an animal or the first fruits of the harvest. The blood sacrifice of an animal in the Old Testament was a foreshadowing of the blood sacrifice of Jesus Christ that covers over one's sins and makes one right with God.

saints—people who believe in God.

Saul—the first king of Israel.

Selah—possibly a liturgical direction inserted into a psalm.

sin—acts that go against God's will; the desire of people's hearts to go against God.

sinfulness—disobedience to God's will; breaking God's law.

sinners—people who disobey God's will as revealed in his Word.

Sirion—another name for Mount Hermon, the most prominent mountain north of Palestine.

Spirit—in the Old Testament, God's animating and life-giving power given to his special servants.

thank offering—a sacrifice given in thankfulness for the blessings of the Lord and usually followed by a festal meal.

transgressions—sins; acts of disobedience to God's will.

unfailing love—special love that forms the basis for covenant relationships.

vows—solemn, religiously binding promises made to God.

wicked—people who are not righteous because they do not follow the Lord.

witness—one who testifies in a court of law to the truth of a situation.

Zion—the city of Jerusalem or, more particularly, the temple and the hill on which the city was built. Sometimes the word indicates the entire "people of God."

Lesson 1

Psalm 104

The God Who Has Made Us

1. ***Psalm 104:1-4***

    a.   What reasons does the psalmist give for praising the Lord?

    b.   What part of creation does the psalmist describe in these verses?

    c.   What images or word pictures does the psalmist use to describe
         God's control of this part of creation?

2. ***Psalm 104:5-9***

    a.   Describe what is happening in these verses.

    b.   How do we see the Lord's control here?

    c.   Do these verses refer to God's actions in the present or in the
         past? How does this contrast with verses 2-4?

3. *Psalm 104:10-18*

    a.   How do the waters benefit the earth?

    b.   How do people and animals benefit?

    c.   What progression in creation do you see between this passage and verses 1-9?

4. *Psalm 104:19-23*

    a.   For what purpose did God create the sun and moon?

    b.   How does the cycle of day and night allow people and animals to coexist in creation?

5. *Psalm 104:24-26*

    a.   What is the relationship between the Lord and creation (v. 24)?

    b.   How do the sea and the life in it demonstrate the Lord's control?

6. *Psalm 104:27-30*

    a.   How does God relate to the creatures in the world?

    b.   How do the animals respond to God's care?

7. *Psalm 104:31-35*

    a.   What is the psalmist's prayer (v. 31) ?

    b.   In what different ways does the psalmist respond to God's work?

8. *Psalm 104*

    a.   As you review this psalm, what word picture would you use to describe God's relationship to the world?

    b.   What does this psalm imply is the role of the human race in God's creation? The role of the animals? Of the rest of creation?

    c.   What would you say is the psalmist's relationship to the Lord?

d.   In what ways has the study of this psalm changed or reinforced your ideas about God?

Lesson 2

Psalms 86 and 116

The God of Compassion

1. *Psalm 86:1-7*

    a.   How does the psalmist describe himself?

    b.   How does he describe the Lord?

    c.   What does he want the Lord to do for him?

2. *Psalm 86:8-10*

    How does the Lord compare to other gods?

3. *Psalm 86:11-13*

    a.   What does the psalmist ask of God?

    b.   What does he promise in return?

4. **Psalm 86:14-17**

   a. Who is attacking the psalmist?

   b. How does the psalmist appeal to God? On what does he base his appeal?

   c. What does the psalmist request of the Lord as he concludes his prayer?

5. **Psalm 116:1-2**

   What general situation does the writer describe in these verses?

6. **Psalm 116:3-6**

   a. In what trouble did the writer find himself?

   b. What did he do to get out of trouble?

   c. Why was the psalmist confident that the Lord would act on his behalf?

d. What happened as a result?

7. *Psalm 116:7-11*

How does the psalmist describe the help he received from the Lord?

8. *Psalm 116:12-19*

a. How does the psalm writer answer his question in verse 12?

b. How does he describe his relationship to God?

9. *Psalms 86 and 116*

In what ways has the Lord shown himself to be a compassionate God?

Lesson 3
Psalms 29, 82, and 146

Our God Reigns

1. *Psalm 29:1-2*

   How are the "mighty ones" to respond to the Lord?

2. *Psalm 29:3-9*
   a. What is the "voice of the LORD" like?

   b. What does the Lord's voice do? What power does it have?

3. *Psalm 29:10-11*
   a. What do these verses tell us about the Lord?

   b. How do God's people benefit from God's rule?

4. *Psalm 82:1*

   What is the setting described in this verse?

5. *Psalm 82:2-7*

   a. What situation has caused God to pronounce judgment?

   b. What does God call those who rule under him to do in order to correct the situation?

   c. What verdict does God pronounce upon the "gods"?

6. *Psalm 82:8*

   Why does the psalmist ask for God's judgment on the earth?

7. *Psalm 146:1-4*

   a. What contrast does the psalmist set up in these verses?

   b. Why does the psalmist warn against putting one's trust in princes?

8. *Psalm 146:5-9*

   Jacob was one of the ancestors of the people of Israel. The phrase "God of Jacob" was one of the names the Israelites used for the Lord God.

   a. What kind of people are described here? Whom does God help?

b. How does God help them?

c. How does the psalmist describe the Lord in these verses?

9. *Psalm 146:10*
   a. What contrast is evident between verse 10 and verses 3-4?

   b. What response does the psalmist call for from the reader? Why is this response appropriate?

10. *Psalms 29, 82, 146*

    According to these psalms, in what ways should we expect to see God's rule revealed in the world?

Lesson 4
Psalms 36 and 103

The God of Unfailing Love

1. *Psalm 36:1-4*

   a. How do these verses describe the "sinfulness of the wicked"?
   What progression do we see here?

   b. What does the psalmist imply is the main cause of this
   sinfulness?

2. *Psalm 36:5-9*

   a. What characteristics of the Lord are described in this passage?

   b. How do the people mentioned in these verses differ from those
   described in verses 1-4?

3. *Psalm 36:10-12*

   a. For what does the psalmist pray?

   b. What is the final end of those who know God? Of the wicked?

4. *Psalm 103:1-6*

   According to these verses, what benefits has the psalmist received from the Lord?

5. *Psalm 103:7-10*

   In what ways has the Lord shown love toward God's people?

6. *Psalm 103:11-13*

   To what does the psalmist compare God's love?

7. *Psalm 103:14-18*

   a.   What does the Lord know about human nature?

   b.   According to verse 18, what does it mean to fear the Lord?

8. *Psalm 103:19-22*

   a.   What position does the Lord occupy in creation?

   b.   Who is called upon to praise the Lord?

9. Psalms 36 and 103

According to these two psalms, how does the Lord show unfailing love to his people?

Lesson 5

Psalms 57 and 33

The Faithful God

1. *Psalm 57:1-3*

    a. On what basis does the psalmist ask for mercy from God?

    b. How does God respond to his request?

2. *Psalm 57:4-6*

    a. In what situation does the psalmist find himself?

    b. What is the final outcome of his predicament?

3. *Psalm 57:7-10*

    a. What does the psalmist promise to do? Why?

    b. How does this passage describe God?

4. **Psalm 57:11**

    With what emphasis does the psalmist conclude this psalm? Why?

5. **Psalm 33:1-3**

    a. How is the Lord to be praised, according to these verses?

    b. How are these verses similar to Psalm 57? How are they different?

6. **Psalm 33:4-5**

    Why is the Lord to be praised?

7. **Psalm 33:6-11**

    a. What has the Lord accomplished through his word? What imagery does the psalmist use to describe this?

    b. How are people to respond to the Lord's work?

    c. What is contrasted in verses 10 and 11? What is the point of this contrast?

8. *Psalm 33:12-19*

   a. Who is blessed, according to these verses? Why is that such a great blessing?

   b. In what should the nations not put their trust? Why not?

   c. What differences do you find between verses 13-15 and 18-19?

9. *Psalm 33:20-22*

   a. What relationship exists between God and his people?

   b. What is their response to the God described in verses 6-19?

   c. What do the people ask for? On what basis do they ask for it?

10. *Psalms 57 and 33*

   According to these psalms, how do God's people experience his faithfulness?

Lesson 6
Psalms 9 and 97

The Lord of Righteousness

1. *Psalm 9:1-2*

   a. What does the psalmist promise God that he will do?

   b. What relationship seems to exist between God and the psalmist? Why would the psalmist make this promise?

2. *Psalm 9:3-6*

   a. What happened to the psalmist's enemies? Why?

   b. On what basis did the Lord take action against the nations?

3. *Psalm 9:7-10*

   a. Describe the Lord's reign. How does it reflect God's righteousness?

   b. What is the Lord's relationship to those who are in need?

4. **Psalm 9:11-12**

   a. What does the psalmist tell his listeners to proclaim about the Lord? Why?

   b. Who is to hear this message?

5. **Psalm 9:13-18**

   a. What does the psalmist want the Lord to do for him?

   b. How does he promise to respond to the Lord?

   c. What contrasts appear in verses 16-18?

   d. Summarize the main point of these verses in your own words.

6. **Psalm 9:19-20**

   What is the psalmist's final prayer? How is it related to the Lord's righteousness?

7. *Psalm 97:1*

How should the earth respond to the Lord's reign?

8. *Psalm 97:2-6*

a. What imagery does the psalmist use to describe the Lord's rule?

b. What do these verses tell us about God?

9. *Psalm 97:7*

How does this verse contrast with verses 1-6?

10. *Psalm 97:8-9*

Why does Zion rejoice?

11. *Psalm 97:10-12*

a. What do those who love the Lord receive?

b. How are God's people to respond to God's rule?

12. Psalms 9 and 97

    a.   How do these two psalms describe God's relationship to creation?

    b.   How is the Lord's righteousness a comfort to those who love him? A threat to those who oppose him?

Lesson 7

Psalm 145

The God Above All Gods

1. ***Psalm 145:1-2***

    a. What words in these verses indicate the mood of this psalm?

    b. Who is to be praised?

2. ***Psalm 145:3-7***

    a. How do these verses describe the Lord?

    b. How will God's people respond to God, according to the psalmist?

3. ***Psalm 145:8-13a***

    a. What characterizes the Lord's relationship to the world?

    b. Who will respond to the Lord? What will they say about God?

c. How does the psalmist describe the Lord's kingdom?

4. *Psalm 145:13b-16*
    a. How does the Lord act toward all creation?

    b. How do God's creatures respond?

5. *Psalm 145:17-20*
    a. What qualities of God do these verses describe?

    b. To whom is the Lord particularly attentive?

    c. What does the Lord do for them?

6. *Psalm 145:21*
    What does the psalmist see as an appropriate response to the Lord's love?

7. *Psalm 145*

    a.   What have you learned about the Lord in this psalm? In this study on the Psalms?

    b.   How would you characterize God's relationship with the world?

    c.   What response do you think is appropriate to such a God?

Lesson 8

Isaiah 55; John 6:35-40; 1 John 1:5-2:2

The God Who Calls Us

1. *Isaiah 55:1-2*

   a. What invitation is given in these verses?

   b. How would you describe the people to whom this invitation is given?

   c. How will the guests benefit by accepting the invitation?

2. *Isaiah 55:3-5*

   a. What promises does God make in these verses?

   b. Why does God make this covenant?

   c. How is God described in these verses?

3. *Isaiah 55:6-7*

    a. What response does Isaiah urge his listeners to make?

    b. How will God respond to those who accept the invitation?

4. *Isaiah 55:8-11*

    a. How is God different from people?

    b. Why are rain and snow good word pictures for God's word?

5. *Isaiah 55:12-13*

    a. What kinds of transformation will take place when people accept God's invitation?

    b. What is the purpose of the sign that God gives?

6. *John 6:35-40*

    a. What connection might this passage have to Isaiah 55:1-2?

b. What is the Father's will, according to verses 39-40?

7. **1 John 1:5-2:2**

    a. How would you characterize God as revealed in this passage?

    b. What happens when people confess their sins? Why does this happen?

    c. What makes it possible for people to walk in the light?

8. **Summary**

    a. How is God's desire for people to come to him demonstrated?

    b. What needs does God supply when we answer his call?

    c. How can we come to God?

    d. How will we be received by God?

Wrap-Up

Listen now to what God is saying to you. You may be aware of things in your life that keep you from coming near to God. You may envision God as unsympathetic, angry, or punishing, although the Scriptures we've studied reveal God's mercy and love. You may feel that you don't know how to pray or come near to God.

Listen to what God is saying to you through Christ Jesus. He is an understanding, loving Father who is calling you now to "come to the waters" (Isaiah 55:1) of spiritual refreshment. God knows firsthand what it's like to live in a sinful, broken world. Jesus has already taken the punishment for your sin, clearing the way for you to come near to God.

Coming near to God is not always easy, but it is simple—as simple as A-B-C:

—**A**dmit that you have sinned and that you need God's forgiveness.
—**B**elieve that God loves you and that Jesus has already paid the price for your sins.
—**C**ommit your life to God in prayer, asking God to forgive your sins, make you his child, and fill you with the Holy Spirit.

Prayer of Commitment

Here is a prayer of commitment to Jesus Christ. If you long to be in a loving relationship with him, pray this prayer. If you have already made that commitment to Jesus, use this prayer for renewal and praise.

"Dear God, I come to you simply and honestly to confess that I have sinned and that sin is a part of who I am. And yet I know that you listen to sinners who are truthful before you. So I come with empty hands and heart, asking for forgiveness.

"I confess that only through faith in Jesus Christ can I come to you. I confess my need for a Savior, and I thank you, Jesus Christ, for dying on the cross to pay the price for my sins. I ask that you forgive my sins and count me among those who are righteous in your sight. Remove all the guilt and stain of my sin.

"Give me your Holy Spirit now to help me pray and to teach me from your Word. Be my faithful God and help me faithfully to serve you. Thank you for loving me. In Jesus' name I pray. Amen."

Evaluation Questionnaire

DISCOVER GOD IN THE PSALMS

As you complete this study, please fill out this questionnaire to help us evaluate the effectiveness of our materials. Please be candid. Thank you.

1. Was this a home group ___ or a church-based ___ program?
   What church?

2. Was the study used for
   ___ a community evangelism group?
   ___ a community grow group?
   ___ a church Bible study group?

3. How would you rate the materials?

Study Guide
   ___ excellent ___ very good ___ good ___ fair ___ poor

Leader Guide
   ___ excellent ___ very good ___ good ___ fair ___ poor

4. What were the strengths?

5. What were the weaknesses?

6. What would you suggest to improve the material?

7. In general, what was the experience of your group?

Your name (optional) _____

Address _____

_____

8. Other comments:

(Please fold, tape, stamp, and mail. Thank you.)

CRC Publications
2850 Kalamazoo Ave. SE
Grand Rapids, MI 49560-0300